Parenting with a Twist

Becoming a *Better* Person Automatically Makes You a *Better Parent*!

DR. BLESSING AKPOFURE, M.D.

COPYRIGHT © 2016 BLESSING AKPOFURE.
ALL RIGHTS RESERVED

ALL RIGHTS RESERVED. NO PART OF THIS
WORK MAY BE REPRODUCED OR STORED
IN AN INFORMATIONAL RETRIEVAL SYSTEM,
WITHOUT THE EXPRESS PERMISSION OF THE
PUBLISHER IN WRITING.

Parenting with a Twist – ISBN: 978-0-9979654-0-7
Library of Congress Control Number: 2016962622

PUBLISHED BY:
SIMPLY GOOD PRESS
WWW.SIMPLYGOODPRESS.COM
MONTCLAIR, NJ USA

CONTENTS

Foreword 1

Introduction 3

Chapter 1: No Regrets 9

Chapter 2: Thank You! 19

Chapter 3: Be In the Now 29

Chapter 4: Be in Your Kids' Now 37

Chapter 5: Be a Parent, Not a Friend! 49

Chapter 6: It Happened to Me 59

Chapter 7: Becoming a Better You 69

Chapter 8: Proven Strategies for Becoming
Your Best Self 73

Bonus 81

Conclusion 83

About the Author 89

Foreword

Whether you are a rookie parent with your first on the way, or you are feeling a little fraught and overwhelmed by your own family (don't worry, this too shall pass), **Parenting with a Twist: Becoming a Better Person Automatically Makes You a Better Parent!** is a book that will give you a fresh new perspective.

Parenting has been described as everything from a thankless chore to a troublesome joy, but what often gets lost in the midst of the diapers, soccer meets and bandaged knees is how much parenting changes you. Your life changes forever the day you look at a child and realize that he or she is yours, and those changes may be deeper, more profound and more wonderful than you think!

In **Parenting with a Twist: Becoming a Better Person Automatically Makes You a Better Parent!** Dr. Blessing offers you a new perspective on the joys of parenthood. Of course being a parent should change you, but why shouldn't it change you for the better and be fun at the same time? Spending time with children means spending time with people who are brand new to the world, and they can give you a kind of guidance that you will never see from someone older or more cynical.

Dr. Blessing takes the lead and asks you the questions that you have always needed to hear, guiding you to answers that will echo through your heart. Life is a series of puzzles that always need to be solved, but with the right help, encouragement and love at your side (the love of a child, and yours, at that); they will slide easily open in your hands.

Have you ever thought that parenting was hard, thankless or nerve-wracking? ***Parenting with a Twist: Becoming a Better Person Automatically Makes You a Better Parent!*** offers you a chance to transcend that paradigm and to learn what it means to be a great parent and a great person, from the perspective of the people that matter the most, your family.

When it is all said and done, nothing matters as much as having the love, support and admiration of your family, especially of your children. In the cycle of life, at some point, the roles reverse. The child becomes the parent and the parent becomes the child and the favor is returned.

— Dennis S. Riff, MD

Introduction

When it comes to the words that I use to describe myself, quite a few pop to mind. I am an educated woman, I am a believer in communication, I am very loving, and above all, I am a parent—"the best mommy in the world," according to my daughter. I must say that this is quite a compliment from a sensitive and insightful being like my daughter. This is why, as an educated woman and physician, the most gratifying job I have ever had is being a parent.

You know you are doing a great job when your child, at age 10, tells you after being scolded that "I thought about it, and I know I could have done better." I was always told that having a child would change everything, but what I didn't know was that it would improve me so much!

In raising my daughter Gabby, several things have become clear to me. Beyond simply performing my duties as a mother, I've realized I need to be a good person if I want to make sure that my child starts out right in life. I used to think that I could be a good mother and that would be enough, but part of being a good mother is being a good person.

As a parent, I also became cognizant of the fact that my parenting skills, or lack thereof, would impact not only my child but all humanity for generations to come, and it was therefore imperative to teach by example. It is not only more authentic, but so much easier to raise a child by example rather than resorting to old standbys like "do as I say, not as I do." The "because I said so" parenting method does not work very well, since children are naturally driven to grow by pushing the envelope and challenging the status quo. They say that "what you resist, persists," and this is as true for raising children as it is for any other area of life.

The more I've thought about it, the more I've realized that I disagree completely with almost every parenting book out there. If you've spent any amount of time looking over these books on the shelves in a bookstore or your local library, you know exactly what I mean. Instead of including yourself in the caretaking equation, many of these books teach you to assess yourself only through the lens of your role as a parent, as if all good parents are poured from the same mold. On the other side of this assumption is the implication that each child will thrive when exposed to the same parenting style, a belief that has no basis in reality.

Just take a moment to observe any playground. Few children are drawn to the same activity, and every kid behaves differently. Don't you think these little diverse individuals deserve more than a cookie-cutter approach to parenting? When it comes to being a parent, it is far more important for you to be a centered and whole person than to master textbook parenting techniques. We cannot and should not all fit into one mold. Life doesn't deal in absolutes, and neither should we.

When I sat down to think about it, and when I discussed this with the people that I've known and the people that I've mentored, my mind kept returning to the same theme: you can't be a good parent without being a complete and happy human being. In another aha moment, I realized that being a complete and happy person is also essential to a fulfilling marriage. Your spouse can never make you happy and complete if you don't do it first. It is up to each of us to learn to give ourselves this gift, so we can approach all our relationships with a full cup.

Having observed my parent friends and their families, I realized that none of them fit into the same "good mom" or "good dad" mold. There are so many parenting styles, but I did notice one theme that seemed to hold true across them all: regardless of their specific beliefs and child-rearing practices, the happiest parents, and the ones with the most outgoing, vibrant and curious children, were the ones who were the most at peace with themselves.

A very important aspect of being a good person is self-care. Please understand that prioritizing self-care is not the same thing as being self-centered. One big aha moment I experienced very early as a parent is that "SELFISH IS A GOOD THING, SELF-CENTERED IS NOT." When Gabby was only 2 weeks old, I ended up in the emergency room with blood pressure high enough to have given me a stroke, due to sleep deprivation.

This sleep deprivation had resulted from me trying to be the super-mom who takes care of everything single-handedly. In the constant doing, I had robbed myself of much-needed rest. My obstetrician pulled me aside and sternly warned me that by not taking care of myself, I was being self-centered and not thinking about my family! If I had a stroke, I would be the one needing care instead of my brand new baby. By putting myself first, I could better ensure that we were both well taken care of.

I can hear the groundswell of protests now: how can ignoring your children in favor of self-fulfillment possibly make you a better person? Isn't it selfish to think of yourself first? Yes, selfish is good, self-centered is bad! Look at yourself in the mirror and say out loud to yourself, "I love me. SELFISH GOOD, SELF-CENTERED BAD."

The world tells us that being selfish is a bad thing, but this is totally wrong.

Self-centered is when it is all about you, it is my way or the highway, and there is no flexibility. Saying "I come first, no matter what the consequences to you," is being self-centered. However, being selfish is saying, "because I love my children, I am taking some 'me time' to rejuvenate, so that when I am with them I am there 100%, both physically and emotionally."

View it this way. When you want to make cookies, you need flour, eggs, sugar, butter, salt, baking powder, and vanilla extract, right? You wouldn't just assume that you could make cookies from flour alone, would you? Of course not, because you know you need all of the ingredients to make a complete and delicious cookie.

You are a complete person, apart from the roles you play in life. You are not just a mother, a colleague, or a marathon runner. You are all these things and more. While I rejoice in my role as a mother, I would play that role poorly if I over-identified with it; I want to model authenticity and wholeness for my daughter, not self-suppression. The more I've come to understand these things, the better parent I've become.

Sometimes I think back to who I was at the time my daughter was born. I remember with fondness how excited I was, and recall with frustration and sorrow some of the beliefs I held and pain that I carried. I think about how hard my life would be if I were still the same person I was then, and indeed, how rough my daughter's life would be as well!

I love the person that I used to be, but I love the person that I've grown into so much more. I came out of my shell, found my true calling, and have helped many people as a result. I know that I am setting an example for my daughter of who an adult can become when she sets her mind to it.

Too many people think that when they have children, their lives must become exclusively devoted to parenting, but this perception is harmful to our children as well as ourselves. What I'm suggesting is that when you define yourself only as a parent, you are limiting yourself and your child by extension. In any relationship, even one as close as that of parent and child, it is very easy to become resentful if you over-identify with your role in it. The question is, can we model self-love and empowerment for and with our children, instead of co-dependency?

When you work to improve yourself, you are guaranteed to become a much better parent. Instead of responding only from your experiences as a parent, you will be able to respond from your experiences as a complete person.

If you are a new parent or will become one soon, take a moment to seriously think about the roles you play in your life. What can you do to help yourself feel more fulfilled? When was the last time you really felt content and happy with your life?

I am not suggesting that parenting should be easy, or that you will find you have tons of time left over for self-improvement or fun after having children. I've known only too well how easy it is to run ragged from morning to night, only to fall into an exhausted sleep before waking up and doing it all over again.

However, my aim in this book is to show you that your growth, your development and your happiness are not fringe benefits to be attended to only after everything else on your list is checked off. Instead, they should be priorities, just like regular doctor's visits and grocery store trips.

Being a better person will make you a better parent. As you work on yourself, you will find a new level of patience and love gently suffusing your relationship with your child. Offer your child the example of a happy and fulfilled parent, and you will be amazed at how they blossom. In this way, you can actually get a second chance to be a child again!

When you free yourself from the mistaken idea that you are a parent and nothing more, it will be as if your eyes have been opened. Instead of seeing the world only through the lens of your role as a parent, you will see everything the world has to offer and all of the joy and the wonder that is really always there. Then you will be able to turn right around and share that with your child, giving them the gift of a positive outlook on life.

When you are fulfilled as a person, you will find that you have tons more energy for life. Instead of just getting through every day, you will relish the thought of what's still to come. You'll step out of bed in the morning with a spring in your step, knowing that you will be your true authentic self today, not someone's cookie-cutter idea of what a parent is.

I'm definitely "mom" to my daughter, but she also knows me as a happy and complete person, one who loves and understands her just as she is. This is one of the most important gifts that I can give her, and it is also one of the most important gifts that I can give myself.

CHAPTER 1

No Regrets

In that moment I understood that the cruelest words in the universe are "if only." LISA SEE

The other day, I was comforting my daughter regarding a disappointment that she had had at school. As I stroked her hair, hugged her and told her that it would be all right, it struck me how much pain she was experiencing.

My daughter is young, and I knew that in a few days she would most likely have forgotten all about what happened. However, in that moment as she sobbed and raged, all I could think about was how terrible it would be if she always felt like this. How difficult life would be if every upset and every disappointment caused us to fall to pieces, downed by carrying the weight of those intense emotions around with us!

Instead, I watched as Gabby picked herself up and got over it. In less than 24 hours, she was playing and laughing again, ironically with the same kids who had upset her the day before. All of her grief and sorrow that had seemed so consuming on Monday was gone by Tuesday. For some reason, the incident stayed with me, and eventually I understood that what I was feeling was awe.

Think about the last time that you disappointed yourself. Maybe you acted out of anger or frustration instead of kindness and love, or perhaps you made a careless mistake due to exhaustion. Maybe you hurt someone, or maybe you simply denied yourself an opportunity that would have changed everything. It happens to everyone.

When I asked you to think about that, there's a good chance that you felt that old shiver of shame and regret. No matter how long ago the incident was, or how much better things got afterward, that regret has stayed with you.

When I watched my daughter get over such an intense upset so quickly, I wished fiercely that I could do the same thing. Like everyone else in the world, I have done things and thought things that I've not been proud of. I have spoken out of turn, I have been quiet when I should have spoken up, I have acted out of self-centeredness, and I have hurt myself and the people around me as a result.

How much better would life be if, after experiencing and doing what we could to resolve any negative situation, we were then able to move forward with no regrets at all? Think about how much more energy we would have, and how much freer our thoughts would be! If we could just let go of the emotional weight we carry, we'd have so much more energy to put towards things that actually matter.

Regret Is a Waste of Time and Energy

I've found there are two things that are important to understand about regret. First, everyone has regrets, and second, they don't matter at all! Regrets are a waste of the time spent dwelling on them, of the physical energy that could have been directed into something more fun, and of the emotional energy that remains stuck in the past.

Did you flinch a little when I said that? You may have even become angry.

Chapter One

Let's get something straight. You have done bad things and you have had bad things done to you— we all have. That is the nature of the world, and it is your right to feel angry at this, and to process it in your own way. However, regrets will not help with that process. Don't stay stuck, but rather resolve to do whatever it takes to move on. Regret locks you in the past, preventing you from fully enjoying the gifts of the present.

Regret happens when your mind fixates on something that happened in the past, gnawing endlessly on it like a dog would gnaw a bone. You think about things that you could have done differently, wonder what the alternatives might have been, and you may even worry about how the choices you made might continue to haunt you in the future. However, even the Bible tells us that worrying does not change anything and is therefore unproductive.

A very wise man once said that the past should be left in the past. It is where you came from, but you cannot return to it and choose differently; you can only make a different choice now. If you try to drag the past forward with you, you are weighing yourself down and slowing your evolution.

Living without regrets is a revolutionary concept for many people. Some even find the idea frightening, because regret has become so central to their identity that they do not know who they are without it! Ask yourself how often you think about your past and become angry or frightened about something that you cannot change.

The truth is that life can only improve when you let go of regret and end those pointless cycles of fear and pain. When you are thinking about regrets, you are not thinking about how to have fun with your child, or how to guide them towards becoming a happy adult.

I'm not saying that getting rid of your regrets is easy. As a matter of fact, it can be quite difficult for some people. However, I will say that no matter how tough it may seem to get rid of your regrets, it will always be easier than you think it is. It's something you have to do one day at a time, putting one foot in front of the other. Pat yourself on the shoulder, and say "good job" every time you catch yourself regretting the past and then mentally cancel that thought. Just having the intention to let go of the past goes a long way. Somewhere deep inside, you are already eager to let go of these harmful thought patterns. As a matter of fact, regret is boring! It is the same thing over and over again, and aren't you tired of hearing it?

Letting go of your regrets is the first step on your journey, but it is so essential. It's my experience that we can't progress when we are hampered by regrets, and this is why we're going to work so hard in this book to free you from the clutches of the past. Acceptance of what is, is the first step to transformation.

Sometimes you look around at other people, at celebrities or even ordinary folks passing you on the street, and you think that surely they do not have regrets. They do not wake up at night replaying embarrassing things that they said or did, and surely they do not have anxiety over things that occurred years ago. To believe that we are the only ones who aren't perfect is as common as it is absurd.

In your mind's eye, others don't seem at all bothered and anxious about stuff that's happened in the past, but the truth is that most people do carry regret, which is a pity for them. But, you don't have to feel that way.

An awful double standard in our culture tells us that we should regret things, but at the same time we should not express our unpleasant feelings. How much happier would we be if we had never been taught that we needed to regret certain choices, but if instead we had been taught that in the eyes of God, there's no such thing as a mistake? If, however, we are taught that regret is sometimes justified, we should also be given safe spaces and structures in which to feel it, express it, and then let it go.

Then we would have a constructive way of dealing with these emotions, and they would no longer pollute our individual and collective emotional space.

Alas, most of us do not grow up in that kind of environment, and that is why we need to heal this in ourselves, so the next generation can put regret in its place.

Everyone has done something that is worthy of regret. Absolutely everyone. People who are amazing, brilliant, bright and clever have regrets. If you think about what you have done and you dwell on the bad stuff, you are sunk! The trick is to learn from our choices and experiences without using them as an excuse to blame others or beat ourselves up.

Giving in to the negative emotions that travel with regret is something that will leave you feeling tired, anxious, and depressed, and in many cases it can even lead to physical illness.

Think of your thoughts as footsteps that leave tracks all over your mind. If you think a particular series of thoughts long enough, these thoughts will leave a groove in your mind, like the track from a big rig truck in the sand. Another word for these grooves is 'beliefs.' That's right, beliefs are just thoughts that you think over and over again. Just like a groove or a rut in the road, beliefs, both conscious and unconscious, make you more likely to stay on the same path. So the more you think a certain way now, the more likely you are to think that way in the future! This can create a vicious cycle if you don't take steps to deal with your limiting beliefs and negative emotions constructively.

Get It All Out In A Safe and Healthy Way

Here is one exercise that you can do if you live near a large body of water. When you feel like you want to get rid of some regrets and other bad energy, make the trip to the water's edge. Bring your child with you if you like, because this is an exercise that can help them as well.

Spend some time gathering small stones or pebbles. Just look for rocks that are light enough to heft but still feel nice and solid in your hand. Pile these rocks next to you on the shore, then pause for a moment. If your child is with you, hold their hand.

Breathe deeply, in and out. Breathe from the bottom of your belly, drawing the air from the innermost core of your being. Take in the fresh clean air, and blow out the old air, revitalizing yourself with every breath.

When you feel calm, pick up the first rock from your pile. Think about a regret you've had, whether it's not going to college, or something cruel you said, or even something unkind that someone has said to you. Hold it in your hand and imagine that instead of the rock, it is this regret that you are holding.

Squeeze the rock in your hand as if you are going to crush it. You are not getting very far, are you?

If you squeeze a rock, it stays a rock, and if you hang on to a regret, it will never be anything but a regret, taking up space in your head and diverting energy from your heart.

When you realize this, fling the rock away from you into the water. Throw it as hard and as far as you can, and watch it sink out of sight. Feel the weight of the rock as it leaves your hand. When the rock strikes the water, observe how the ripples grow larger and larger before disappearing entirely.

Repeat this process until you have dealt with all the regrets that you can think of. Concentrating on the regret and the physical feeling of flinging it away can leave you feeling tired or empty, but it will also leave you feeling free and clean.

This is a great practice to share with your child, because it teaches them that after they have done everything they can to fix an issue, they need to move on with their lives. It gives them a healthy way to look at themselves and life, and helps them realize that they can be purposeful about their thoughts, just as you can be purposeful about yours. It is fun being a child again, even when it comes with the responsibilities of being a parent.

Do you remember that belief rut we talked about before? Right now, you need to teach your brain a new way to think. This is not easy, but it is something that can help you so, so much.

For example, say that you regret losing your temper at someone who was very close to you. Maybe that friendship or relationship has never recovered. You may be plagued with frequent thoughts of regret surrounding that incident.

The next time you have those thoughts, try to interrupt them by thinking, "Hey! There's nothing I can do to change that! I apologized, and now I need to move on with my life." Everything happens for a reason; there must have been a good reason for any experience to unfold the way it did. Oh well, happy, happy, joy, joy." Those are the affirmations I use to disrupt a negative train of thought. I'm sure you can just as easily come up with ones that are meaningful to you

Some people lean on repeating statements like "The past is the past; I don't have time for regrets." The point is to do whatever it takes to get your brain out of the habit of thinking regretful thoughts. When you do this, you heal yourself as well as future generations.

I've put together some quotes to inspire and to move you out of regret through forgiveness when you find yourself languishing in the past. This may include forgiving others or forgiving yourself.

1. "The weak can never forgive. Forgiveness is the attribute of the strong." — Mahatma Gandhi
2. "Forgiveness does not change the past, but it does enlarge the future." — Paul Boose
3. "Forgiving does not erase the bitter past. A healed memory is not a deleted memory. Instead, forgiving what we cannot forget creates a new way to remember. We change the memory of our past into a hope for our future." — Louis B. Smedes
4. "The practice of forgiveness is our most important contribution to the healing of the world." — Marianne Williamson
5. "True forgiveness is not an action after the fact, it is an attitude with which you enter each moment." — David Ridge
6. "True forgiveness is when you can say 'Thank you for that experience'." — Oprah Winfrey

My favorite is Oprah's quote. By dwelling in regret and pain, you lose the blessing of the lesson. Only when you find it within yourself to forgive whoever has offended or pained you, can you grow.

Some of you may question how it is that I can possibly understand the extreme pain you've gone through, especially if you've been subjected to domestic violence or abuse. Here is a confession– I have gone down that road too. I was physically and sexually abused as a child and vowed that my own daughter would be loved, protected and respected to the best of my ability. It was my own experience of abuse that has made me a better mother to my child. Even though I suffered emotional and physical pain growing up, I have moved on, and am offering my child the safe haven and protection that she needs, at any time of the day.

The childhood abuse left me with another legacy. I am driven to succeed because I promised myself that I would never leave myself so weakened as to be taken advantage of by another ever again. I also learned to forgive myself and to forgive the offenders, even if they, when confronted, denied abusing me. It was as if their memory banks had been wiped clean of any recall of the atrocities. Whether it was from guilt or denial, it doesn't matter. Their fervent denials did leave me wondering if I had imagined everything, and, for a little while, I doubted the veracity of my own memories. Of course, I wasn't wrong, and I had to forgive myself for even questioning or doubting my own pain.

I decided to view my unhappy upbringing as a gift. When I finally spoke up about it to my family, some deeply hidden secrets were forced out of the closet at the same time. It was a revelation that so much abuse lay hidden, ignored and overlooked. I was branded a black sheep for having had the audacity and courage to speak up. Well, I have to say I am a very happy black sheep. I don't live in regret, I've forgiven and left the pain behind, and I've reshaped my life.

"The Ocean" by Gabrielle Latimore, Age 6

18   Parenting with a Twist

CHAPTER 2

Thank You!

I would maintain that thanks are the highest form of thought, and that gratitude is happiness doubled by wonder. GILBERT K. CHESTERTON

When we were very young children, we were taught by our parents and other adults to say thank you in order to be polite. This is an important way to grease society's wheels by showing that we are civilized human beings who are grateful for the work and efforts of others on our behalf. Indeed, placing value on gratitude in this way is at the core of cultures across the world, and it is passed on from parent to child. There is a joy that fills you when your child expresses gratitude to you that makes you want to do even more for them. And believe me, they can also get a lot out of you by being thankfully cute!

In some cultures, people express gratitude directly, while in others, it is conveyed more subtly through gifts and gestures. If you were raised in a multi-cultural household or community, you might be conversant with several different ways of expressing gratitude. "Thank you" is one of the most important phrases we can learn to say, and it makes sense that in beginning language courses, it is one of the first things that we are taught.

Try this exercise. Over the next week, make the effort to thank anyone you encounter from a different culture, in their native language. It is amazing to see how they light up in appreciation when you make the effort to express a few words of thanks in the language of their birth. Just like that, they become more receptive and more welcoming of you, because you cared enough to try.

However, no matter how good you are at saying thank you to the people who deserve it, there is one individual who probably never hears you say it often enough, and that is yourself. You are a unique and singular human being, and I would lay a wager that you have never thanked yourself for being so special.

The Mechanism of Thanks

Why do we thank people? There are the reasons that I have listed above, but in reality, the concept of thanks is a two-way street. When you thank someone for their work, you are acknowledging them and letting them know that you recognize what they have done.

However, it is important to understand that something fascinating happens when we are on the receiving end of gratitude. We are social creatures in any case, but something about being thanked makes us shine. Although placing excessive importance on receiving thanks and praise might be dysfunctional, being sincerely thanked triggers positive emotions and the release of beneficial brain chemicals. This binds us to other people, making us feel that we are not only part of a group, but also a part of a family.

It feels really fantastically great to be appreciated.

In families where expressing thanks to one another is not an ingrained habit, deep emotional issues can arise. Most obviously, people in those circumstances tend to feel consistently under-appreciated. That feeling of under-appreciation is dangerous for everyone. With younger people, there is the possibility that they will feel adrift, as if they do not have direction. With older people, they may feel neglected or burdensome. A lack of gratitude can cause all involved to feel used and abused, which eventually builds resentment even between couples.

As we can see, there are many, many reasons why saying thank you is so important. Why, then, does it always feel like such a shock when we are thanked? My guess is that it is because we are never thanked enough, and for some of the most important things in our lives, we are never thanked at all!

When you think about thanks, you often think about grateful sentiments traveling from you to another person, but I suggest that you think about it the other way as well. You must think of gratitude as coming back to you and settling on your shoulders. You need and deserve that validation. There is no shame in it, and there is a great deal of growth that can come about from acknowledging all there is to be grateful for about yourself.

Let Me Thank You

I do not know much about you. All I know is that you stopped to pick up my book, and that you've liked what you found here enough to keep reading this far. You may have felt beleaguered in the past. You may have felt as if life has taken things from you, but lo and behold, you're still here. Some days, you feel as if you could be swept away, but for reasons you may not fully understand, you have hung on.

There may have been days when it felt as if it would be easier to let yourself get swept away, but there was always something that kept you hanging on. If you are anything like me, it was the thought of your precious child that kept you going, the same being who inspired you to pick up this book in the first place. Perhaps it was simply your love for them that kept you from falling over that edge, or your sense of duty or responsibility towards them. In any case, you had the motivation you needed to overcome obstacles and arrive where you are standing right now.

I can see that you are someone who still has doubts and fears. Maybe, in the dark of night, you castigate yourself for what you think of as a weakness. Let me remind you, however, that fear is something that is essential to our survival. It tells us when things are wrong, or when we are in danger. No one is lucky enough to go through his or her entire life without danger. What you have accomplished is that you have survived everything in your life up until this point. You have weathered storms in the form of people who didn't have your best interests at heart, dashed hopes and much, much more.

You are still here, and I am grateful for your presence on this planet. I am grateful to have someone as fascinating, unique and amazing as you in the world. If it feels like I am being a little over-exuberant in my praise, don't worry about it. In some very small way, I am just trying to make up for the years that you have toiled without thanks, for all the times that you have worked so hard, only to have people turn their backs on you and offer you nothing in return.

It is wrong for the world not to recognize you for the wonder that you are, and I am just trying to do what I can to fix it. When you feel tired, or when you fall into despair, come back and read these words. You have done good work, and you are worthy of love and gratitude. It is as simple as that.

Thanking Yourself

Did you feel a pleasurable glow warm your insides when you read that last section? Many of us are hungry, indeed are starving, for thanks. The world often does not provide it, and social conditioning tells us that it is not something that we can legitimately seek out from others. It is a hard truth to hear, but the world can be quite harsh for those who look for thanks. After all, when we talk about something difficult or trying, don't we often call it a "thankless task"?

This is where I want you to examine how you might 'rewire' yourself. If something we need does not come from without, it needs to come from within. Or, as Neale Donald Walsch, author of *Conversations With God*, says: "If you don't go within, you'll go without." It is so hard for many people, women especially, to admit that they need to be acknowledged for the work they have done and the struggles they have endured. It can feel self-aggrandizing or dangerous or prideful. However, when you do this, you are merely asking for what is due to anyone who tries to be the best person they can. You are not only asking for monetary reward or to have your own desires satisfied, but you are also asking for the emotional satisfaction that comes with receiving gratitude for all that you do and all that you are.

That is why I am going to instruct you on how to thank yourself. Some of my life-coaching clients burst into nervous laughter when we come to this point. I simply wait it out, then ask them to explain to me why the idea of expressing gratitude to themselves is so silly. When they can't explain, I smile and teach them how important it is to give thanks for yourself.

Stand in front of a mirror, taking long, deep breaths. Do not hold your breath; instead, take it in and let it out slowly. Meet your eyes in the glass, and hold your own gaze steadily for several seconds. Clear your throat, pat yourself on the shoulder, give yourself a hug and say softly, but clearly, "Thank you."

This is enough for some people, but most people, especially at the beginning, need a little more. They wonder what they are thanking themselves for, and sometimes they feel a little too silly to proceed. For this reason, I often give a list of suggestions and ideas. If you are feeling nervous, just try reading a few of these off.

*Thank you for being fantastic!

*Thank you for your patience!

*Thank you for your kindness!

*Thank you for trying so hard!

*Thank you for not giving up!

*Thank you for being here!

*Thank you for everything you do!

*Thank you for being so strong!

*Thank you for being so tough!

*Thank you for your time!

*Thank you for _____!

Fill in the final blank with a phrase that fills your heart with pride, or that makes you feel good about yourself. Simply that feeling of pleasure is worth overcoming your resistance to this process.

Do this exercise every day if possible. It'll feel a little ridiculous at first, but with practice, you will find yourself filled with gladness and warmth every time you do it. You are, in essence, acknowledging the divine treasure you really are.

Deserving Thanks

Sometimes, when I thank someone openly and sincerely for something that they have done, they shrug me off and shake their heads. They tell me that it really was not a big deal or did not cost them anything, when I know that they really made an effort for me.

The truth is that the world tells us we should not need to be thanked, that we should offer ourselves to all who ask without expectation of return. However, the problem is that when we deny ourselves the opportunity to receive gratitude, it makes us feel unworthy and unappreciated. Some people worry that by accepting thanks, they will be seen as vain or as selfish, when in fact the opposite is true.

This is my challenge to you. The next time someone says thank you to you, simply smile and say, "You're welcome!"

This may sound simple, but when I have my clients try it, they often end up flailing. They instinctively reach for words of dismissal and try to shrug off the gratitude. I hear a lot of the same negations over and over again:

"No, no, it's just fine!"

"Oh, it wasn't a big deal at all."

"You don't have to say anything like that!"

These attitudes make the thing that they did seem lesser, and in many cases, it can make the person who is doing the thanking feel as if their opinion is not validated. In some cases, it can even make the recipients of your good deeds feel bad about themselves!

Think about it. If someone has the courage to come and ask you for help, or when you have done something extraordinary for them, they feel very grateful to you and grateful for your actions.

However, when you tell them that your work for them or your efforts were "nothing much" or "no big deal," they will start to feel as if perhaps you were helping them with something that they should have been able to handle on their own.

Do not diminish their courage in asking for help, and do your best to honor your own work as well. There has never been a better time for you to think about what you do and how your efforts help others.

You deserve thanks for this, and if you do not think you do, you are shortchanging yourself and underestimating your infinite value as a human being.

In the entire universe you are a singular being, here to offer gifts that no one else can. You have a unique energetic signature, and the world would be the poorer if that signature didn't exist. Please be grateful for yourself, because I know that I am grateful that you are here, just as I am grateful for my own existence. I am really thankful for who I am, for the joys as well as the messes in my life. It is often said that "sometimes, out of the messes, you get a message, and out of the tests and struggles, you get a testimony." So, here I go: "I, Dr. Blessing, thank me for being a strong, unique person and for not running away from all my messes." That said, please understand that when I was going through these messes, I was anything but thankful!

Life can be taxing, but here you are. You are magnificent, you are amazing, and you should be so grateful to yourself for what you have accomplished. Recognize that with each expression of gratitude for who you are, for what you have and for the people who support you, by your very acts, posture and attitude, you are teaching a priceless life lesson to your children. You are teaching them that they, too, are worthy beings with valuable gifts to offer, and you are teaching them the joys of both giving and receiving gratitude.

Chapter Two   27

"Watermelon" by Gabrielle Latimore, Age 6

28   Parenting with a Twist

CHAPTER 3

Be In the Now

Your success and happiness lies in you. Resolve to keep happy, and your joy and you shall form an invincible host against difficulties. HELEN KELLER

The great philosophers tell us that there is no time like the present, but I would take that a little farther. There is no time like the present, because it will never be here ever again. The time that we are given on this little planet is precious and finite, and if you want to improve yourself and to truly see the world for what it is, you need to learn about being in the now.

There are people who fail to notice that time flies. Then one day they wake up and realize that their children are grown, and they have no idea how they have ended up with the lives they are now living. When this happens, it is because they have spent all of their time looking down at the ground in front of them, or ahead to some lofty, distant goal, or behind them at the past.

They have never brought their attention into the now, and this tragedy can haunt them for the rest of their lives.

I firmly believe in living in the now, thereby fully inhabiting your body, your mind and your soul. This type of awareness is something that will bring you a great deal of joy and understanding of who you are. If it feels somewhat uncomfortable at first, this is only because presence has not been your norm — just do your best! One of the joys of parenthood is that kids have this uncanny ability to bring you into the now. Below is a transcript of an interaction between Gabby and I that is typical of exchanges between us:

Kid: Mom, Mom!

Mom: What?

Kid: I love you!

She calls me with a sense of urgency, and I turn around thinking *what in heaven's name could be wrong?*

I spin around in a panic, turning away from the writing I am doing, the news show I am watching, the carrots I am cutting for dinner. Suddenly everything that I was worried about before disappears in the face of concern for my child.

Pivoting sharply, I see my lovely daughter standing with her hands on her hips and a big smile on her face. Then she says she loves me, and it just makes me melt. It reminds me that in the middle of all of my big adult worries, all that really matters is how much we care about each other.

Every time she does this, I fall for it. I know she'll probably grow out of it soon, but frankly, I don't even want to think about that day. Just writing about it right now puts a smile on my face, and I can feel my heart glow with love for the wonderful little girl who I get to watch as she learns to love, grow and play.

In that moment, when my daughter's urgent cry pierces my consciousness, I am jerked away from my musings and regrets about the past and my worries and plans for the future. My daughter has reminded me in a way that no guru or spiritual leader ever has that this moment is all we ever really have. Time is a river flowing by, and I must keep my attention in the now if I want to fully drink in the richness of life.

When my daughter does this, she gives me a blinding shock that feels like I have stepped into a wonderfully cool brook on a hot summer day. I sense all my perceptions sharpening. It's as if the world at large has faded away, leaving me aware only that everything that matters in my world is standing there, smiling at me and telling me she loves me.

It is a wonderful break in the middle of what might have been a very tense day, and it is so beautiful.

As an adult, it can be challenging to be in the now. Your best teachers are kids, and if you have none of your own, go to the park and watch other people's children play. Another opportunity to practice being in the now is when you are driving, as you appreciate all the sights that pass you by.

A Meditation on Being In the Present

I would like you to try a meditation that I practice with my clients from time to time. It's a great exercise when you are feeling too rushed, hurried or worried, and many of my clients continue to use it as a grounding technique. It can be quite soothing, and it is designed to help you become one with this moment in which you now find yourself.

Find a space where you will be undisturbed for just a few moments. I know that when you are tending little ones this can be difficult, but it is okay to take a little break. Even just hiding in the bathroom for a minute will do the trick; you do not need to take long!

When you have found a moment of peace, with a door between yourself and the rest of the intrusive world, take a deep breath and close your eyes. Keep yourself as still and steady as you can, and take three very deliberate breaths.

Once you have breathed in peace and breathed out your inner discord, start using your senses to the best of their ability. Feel the ground through your feet, smell the air around you, feel the texture of your clothes between your fingers. Lick your lips, and feel whether they are dry or soft, listen for the drip of water, the sound of children at play or the song of birds.

Interestingly enough, when you close your eyes, you are making the world a great deal bigger. Suddenly, you are using all of your senses to really experience the moment that you are in, the true now of what you are going through. In that same moment, you will realize how small everything is that you have been worried about. The world is great, and you are small, and everything is contained in this simple moment.

There is no moment exactly like this one in all eternity. You will never be in this now again, and when you pay attention to it, you are making the most of your precious time on Earth.

When you open your eyes, thank yourself quietly for taking this moment, and start over refreshed and renewed. This exercise places you squarely in the moment, and it offers you just the kind of pleasure that the moment wishes to give you.

A Jar Full Of Love

A lot of people look down on the trend of taking pictures everywhere they go. They scoff at the idea that every moment needs to be commemorated and then shared. I do not agree! I am a huge fan of the selfie culture, and of Instagram and Facebook postings of meals and food. Instead of seeing a trend for self-centered behavior or self-absorption, what I see is thousands of people recognizing that the moment that they are in is precious and striving to recognize it and to cherish it.

Chapter Three 33

One thing we learn from this kind of culture is that it does not take a lot to make a moment special. It can simply be the fact that you like your hair today, or that your meal is beautiful. Maybe the sky is that special cerulean shade, or perhaps your child's smile is just too precious.

While you can certainly capture your lovely moments via your smartphone, there is a more tactile way to do it as well. For this exercise, all you need is a jar and slips of paper. Whenever you think of a moment that you want to treasure, write down a few words to jog your memory, fold the slip, and throw it into the jar.

I recommend adding one slip to the jar every day. Some of my clients protest, saying that memorable moments do not happen every day. I explain to them that there are memorable moments all around us; we just need to look for them. Sometimes they argue with me, but I am very firm. I send them home to try it for a week or two, and when they come back, they have a fresh perspective.

Things are special and distinct because we want them to be, and in part that is because we are special. A tree growing in the forest with beautiful crimson leaves and a twisted trunk is lovely because we are looking at it. Nothing recognizes beauty the way that a human being does. It is up to you and me to recognize something so rare and precious, and to preserve it.

Work on filling your jar with good things. I keep one myself, and I try to make sure that there is something to add every day. Someday, when I am an old woman, I will have jars full of amazing memories and scattered moments to look back on.

If you need some inspiration, here are some of the things that I have added to my own jar.

Went to horticulture show today. Gorgeous red and gold tulips! Daughter's smile after she showed me her A+

First warm day of spring, went for walk

Daughter's first day back at school, she's so excited! (I'll 'fess up here; I'm known to break out into the happy "back to school" dance.)

Painted nails magenta today

We might not call any of these things life-changing, but I like to think of them as life-defining. If I look at a calendar, all I see are squares and numbers. This is a stultifying way to look at things. If life were really just a series of numbers and straight lines, I wouldn't blame anyone for being confused and convinced of how dull everything was!

However, when I look at my jar, filled with slips of paper that remind me how truly precious it all is, I feel invigorated. I know that there are some beautiful memories behind me, and that there are many, many more that are looking to be made. Not only does this comfort me, but it also draws me higher and higher, allowing me to breathe in the true bliss that surrounds me.

What We Learn From Our Children

Children are masters of being in the now. They feel every moment intensely, and it is only when they grow up that they lose this. Honor your child's place in the world, and remember that for them, everything is focused with diamond precision on this moment.

That means that their joy is intense, but so are their discomforts and their sorrows. When your child's entire being is focused on an itchy tag in their clothing or a certain taste that they cannot tolerate, be willing to recognize this for what it is. Just as stopping to focus on a moment brings it into sharp relief for you, their awareness of the now makes everything more intense for them.

One of my friends used to have an issue with her daughter, who it seemed was a very, very picky eater. Meal times were always a chore as mother and daughter squared off over various foods and meals. Sometimes, days would go by where peace would reign, then suddenly her daughter would be on the verge of tears because there was an item on her plate that she just could not eat.

When my friend came to me for advice about this issue, I had her make up a list of the foods that her child had refused to eat. As it turned out, they were all foods that had fairly strong tastes.

I explained to my friend that children taste things differently from adults. Flavors are very intense for them, and some people, called super tasters, extract more flavor from foods that seem quite bland to others. To them, the taste of food can be too concentrated or too powerful. My friend did not realize that the foods she had thought tasty were causing her daughter a great deal of misery!

She went on to read a few books on taste and super tasters, and now she can prepare meals that are both nutritious and mindful of her daughter's capabilities and preferences.

Be patient with your children when it feels like they are fussing over small details. A child's increased sensitivity and awareness cause feelings to run very intensely through them, taking more energy out of them than the same feelings might us.

Let your child guide you as you learn more about experiencing the now as it is, and use this knowledge to guide them in turn as they develop in their understanding of how the world works. Show them that the world does not have to be as intense as they are, and that they can process immediate sensations using rational thought. In many ways, you will each be teaching each other.

Your child is a source of wisdom, and by being in the now, you are honoring their experience of the world. While a parent's role as teacher is unquestioned remember that you are also a student. Your university is the world, and sometimes the greatest teachers come in the smallest packages. Inventor and futurist Buckminster Fuller said that "our children are our elders in Universe time." Look at your child, and realize that they hold secrets and wisdom that you may have forgotten long ago.

Through mutual love and respect, you and your children will come to a better understanding of each other over time. This is only a small part of being a better adult, but it is essential. Learn from your child what it is to be in the now, and you will find that your eyes have been opened to a whole new world of benevolence, beauty and love.

"Panda Chewing Bamboo" by Gabrielle Latimore, Age 6

CHAPTER 4

Be in Your Kids' Now

Children are likely to live up to what you believe of them. LADY BIRD JOHNSON

We worry about our children's safety, their health and their school grades. Yet we overlook the fact that one of the most powerful ways to get them thinking and learning in rich and complex ways is through shared thinking and conversations as they play.

At a recent lunch with a friend, I noticed that she looked rather stressed and tired. I asked her what was up, and after some thought she told me that it was her kids.

"Every time I look over at them, they're on the computer," she said. "They're playing their game, and when I look over their shoulders, it always looks like the same thing over and over again. I swear, it's like they become zombies when that log-in screen comes on!"

She sounded genuinely distressed, and I was worried she was resorting to high-tech stalking to keep track of her kids.

"Are they falling behind on their schoolwork?" I asked gently. "Have they stopped going out with their friends?"

She answered no, and I shook my head.

"It doesn't sound like you have anything to worry about," I told her. "It sounds like your kids are just using this game to blow off a little steam. So what if they whine a little for another ten minutes when you call them to dinner?"

"I just don't understand," she said. "How can they be that obsessed with animations on a screen for hours on end?'

"Well, why don't you sit down and ask them to show you?"

To make a long story short, my friend eventually decided that she enjoys the game enough to join her kids in it, and now she understands exactly why they think it's so much fun.

"It's kind of addictive," she admits, "but it lets me talk with them and have fun with them."

Children and Focus

The friend whose story I just told discovered something that I've been saying for a while now. Children have their own sense of time, and their ability to focus for long periods on seemingly trivial things can be a little puzzling to adults. Anyone who claims that children have short attention spans hasn't really watched a child play intently with crayons, build mud pies or read their favorite book. When a child's passion is fully engaged, there is virtually no limit to the amount of time they can spend focusing.

I question the frequent diagnosis of attention deficit disorder (ADD) and wonder whether it is sometimes used by society to avoid dealing with the root of the issue. If I had to speculate as to the origins of this problem, I would say that very often, we as adults are unwilling and unable to bridge the gap between our way of being and that of creative children, who are always in the now. Because we are so seldom fully present ourselves, we find it easier to deal with people whose behaviors are predictable and who are easily directed and controlled. So much for thinking outside the box.

It is only as we grow older that we lose the ability to hyper-focus like this. I sometimes feel a painful sense of loss at not being able to engage with life as wholeheartedly as I did when I was a kid. Do you remember the first movie or book that really captured you, drawing you into its imaginary world? I recall spending an entire summer watching my favorite movie over and over again, until I could quote it word for word. My parents wondered what I saw in it, much as the friend I mentioned wondered what her children saw in their video game.

If my parents had asked me why the movie so enthralled me instead of glancing at me disapprovingly over their shoulders, I think I could have willingly and easily shared my interests with them. There was something magical about watching it for me and I was so entranced that even though I knew every line by heart, it never got old.

I'm not sure that I've watched a movie with that kind of avid absorption since I became a teenager. To be honest, sometimes I miss being transported so fully and easily to a different dimension.

The smallest things can forever sway the way that we look at the world. It might be a poem, a book, a movie, a TV show, a comic book, a favorite squeeze toy. These influences enter our lives in the most random fashion. Our interactions with them, planned or unplanned, allow us to feel as if the universe is offering us little pieces of magic just through our being present to the moment.

When I watch my own daughter immersed in play, a book or her favorite video game, I envy her ability to get so engrossed in something wonderful and captivating. It reminds me of when I used to be able to do the same, such as when I read Greek mythology for the first time and it was so vivid that I imagined being there with the gods and goddesses. Those moments have made me ask how I can regain that enthusiasm and focus that came so easily when I was young. What I'm learning is that, as with so many things, the answer has a great deal to do with presence.

Why You Need to Know Your Children's Now

Ultimately, time is a mental construct, and the present moment is all there ever is. Because children are not yet as mentally rigid as adults, they operate on their own understanding of time, and being in the here and now is of great significance to them. For example, an adult knows that lunch happens around noon, but a young child yells and screams when she wants food at 10 a.m. She is not being rude; she is only responding to the hunger pangs in her tummy. That big round thing on the wall with the moving lines, otherwise known as a clock, doesn't have anything to do with the fact that she wants a snack!

This is a very simple example, but if you really internalize this insight, it will help you make much more sense out of your children's behavior. A child's sense of time and priorities is very different from an adult's. This explains why a child is always the first out the door for a zoo visit, but slow as a sloth when you are going to visit a boring relative!

When your child focuses on something, whether it is a game or an interesting bug, learning and development are happening. Understanding this creates several benefits for the parent.

For example, you will be on hand to nurture any interests that your child may be expressing, perhaps by taking a kid who is obsessed with bugs to a butterfly house. You never know when exploring a childhood interest will spark a lifetime passion or even a career!

Bear in mind, of course, that you must always consider your child's safety. In this day and age, most children have access to the computer, but I never think it is a good idea to let your child roam the internet unsupervised. Be aware of why your child is spending so much time on social networking, because chatting with friends is fine and good, but there are bullies and predators out there too.

The point is that an involved parent will not be caught flat-footed by any nasty surprises. If you know what is going on with your child, you will be able to head off trouble at the pass.

Joining your child in his or her experience of now is a great way to bond with them. For children every moment is a learning experience, but often as adults, we expect our kids to see the world on our terms. When you join them in their now, however, they feel safe, supported and secure in a world which is completely of their own design. This is laying the foundation for future happiness and success. Not only that, you will find yourself discovering a whole new perspective as well. Looking at the world through the eyes of a four- or six-year-old offers a tremendously refreshing dose of perspective.

I recently came across a disturbing statistic. According to a March 2014 report from non-profit organization Child Trends, parents are feeling more irritated with their children now than they have in the past. In the US between 1997-2007, the percentage of parents who reported feeling irritation rose from 20% to 35%, and this statistic has remained unchanged since. High levels of parental stress negatively affect children's health, academic success, and sense of psychological and social well-being.

There are a number of reasons why parents have experienced an increase in stress— greater economic insecurity, changes in family structure, the pressure on both parents to work, plus the emergence of the on-demand generation, which is used to getting what they want right now. The bottom line is, parents must make a greater effort to manage stress and nip it in the bud where possible, if they want to be able to join their children in appreciation of their now.

The many benefits of participating in your kid's now go beyond just one generation. When you are present with your kids, you establish a precedent that they will emulate when they have children of their own. It is crucial that this tone be established at a very early stage in your child's life, so it becomes for them a norm and not an intrusion. In this big wild world, children need to have a safe haven, and that should be your role as the parent: to create a place where they feel they belong and where they can be themselves, without fear of judgment or criticism.

You, as the parent, can and should be your child's closest confidant, but it will most likely require some work for you to be granted this privilege. This is because your kids will only feel safe to confide in you when you have worked to become the clear and compassionate presence they want and need. The "because I said so and this is the way my parents did it" approach will not cut it with this generation any more than it did with past ones.

Being Invited In

You have to be invited to join your children in their now, or they may see your presence as intrusive. This is especially true if you have brushed off their invitations to join them in the past. When it comes to my daughter, I have discovered that honesty is invariably the best policy, so I always ask directly.

This may feel a little strange for parents who are used to telling, not asking. For example, children may not really have an opinion on clothing when it is something that their mother or father has always taken care of. Then when they are given a choice, everything suddenly becomes very intense! I've had my daughter say yes to my choice of her clothes for the day, but when I ask her to choose between two different-colored hair ties, the world must grind to a stop as she weighs her options.

I never insist that my child include me. Instead, I ask, and if she says yes, it is a delightful shared experience.

No matter how old your child is, why not make it a point to share their passion and their now with them?

"You really seem to love that video game," you might say. "Can you show me how to play?"

"What a cool drawing! Can you teach me how to draw that?"

"I'm curious about the book you're reading. Can you tell me about it?"

"Wow, you are so good at that. I would love to be able to do that just like you."

You are not questioning their passion or belittling them for enjoying something that they love when you ask these things. Rather, you are demonstrating a keenness to get involved. You are expressing a genuine desire to connect in a way that is meaningful, and which promotes a sense of shared achievement. In such a relationship our children can thrive and gain the confidence they need to explore further.

I have found that this works well when the child is very young. At young and tender ages, children have enormous, trusting hearts that have not yet been dented or hurt. If you ask to be included, they will willingly share everything with you.

Another reason to do this with young children is because it teaches them about limits. As a parent, you have a right to make decisions based on your child's health and safety. However, if you give them the power to accept or refuse your participation in something that is uniquely theirs, you are teaching them to respect their own boundaries. You are creating decision- making experiences for them, and giving them the chance to relate (or not) to others. This is a great way to show them that they are their own people!

With older children, the conversation may be more measured, particularly if you have a history of parent-child disagreements. In this case, they may be sensitive to your disapproval and misread your reasons for suddenly taking an interest in their lives. Once again, though, honesty is the best policy.

"I just want to share something with you and learn more about the things that you love."

Say this with sincerity, and you'll have a better shot at getting past their defenses. Even if you have had a contentious relationship previously, demonstrating a genuine desire to connect can greatly improve the quality of your interactions.

In our community are a man and his son who couldn't be more different from each other. The father is a quiet bookish sort, who spends most of his free time reading and researching. He teaches English at a local college, and his favorite pastime is to organize poetry readings. His son, on the other hand, is a star football player and an extreme extrovert. He is charismatic and loves being the center of attention. He thrives on the attention of his growing number of adoring fans.

Without a doubt, they have had their differences. As with so many father-son relationships, they risked drifting apart as the boy grew older, without common interests to bind them together.

However, everything changed the day the father started attending his son's football games. No matter his schedule or the weather, he made sure he was there to cheer on his son. What's more, he lent his considerable intellect to figuring out the intricacies of the game in order to understand why his son loved it so much. Instead of dismissing his son's accomplishments as the inconsequential achievements of a jock, he invested time and effort into understanding why the sport mattered so much to his boy. For his part, what did the young football player feel when he saw his father in the stands? A fierce joy and pride. This is how you construct durable and long-lasting connections with your children.

I am not saying that this is always easy or simple. On many occasions, time and work are required to rebuild the bridge between parent and child, but the important thing is to start now.

Do not expect your child to take the initiative! So many parents are surprised and disappointed when their children are not perfect carbon copies of themselves. Newsflash: your kids are not you, and the pressures they face are totally different from what you had to deal with in your youth. Your children are unique, wonderful people with their own interests, and they look to you for unconditional love and approval regardless of the differences between you.

Simply reaching out to learn more about your children and what they love will make a huge difference to your relationship with them. The effort you make may instantly add a new dimension to your parent-child connection, or it may require weeks or even months of patient effort.

No matter what, do not give up! As parents, we have this enormously powerful draw to our children. They are born into this world needing us for everything, and even when they are angry, distracted, depressed or distant, as a parent it is your responsibility to provide them with a sense of stability, home and belonging.

Getting Into Your Child's Now

Sometimes it's hard to get involved in your child's interests. After all, our children are not us, and the world they're growing up in is entirely different from the one that we faced as kids.

When your child is showing you something in their now, be fully present for them. Do not fret about errands that must be completed, and do not keep checking your watch or your emails. There is no such thing as time wasted when you are present with your child. You are making time for your child, and you are spending it together in a way that enriches and fulfills you both. Can you recall a time when you fully engaged with your child in this way?

In a piece called "The Creativity Crisis" by educational psychologist Kyung-Hee Kim that was published in a 2011 edition of the Creative Research Journal, Kim notes that a study of schoolchildren from kindergarten to 12th grade shows a broad decline in measures of creativity. Children were found to have become "less emotionally expressive, less energetic, less talkative and verbally expressive, less humorous, less imaginative, less unconventional, less lively and passionate, less perceptive, less apt to connect seemingly irrelevant angles, less synthesizing, and less likely to see things from a different angle" as they grew older.

I have found that by interacting with my child at his or her own pace in a situation where we can learn together and share respect and trust, I am profoundly reinforcing my child's learning ability. That is how a tiny acorn grows into a mighty oak tree: the acorn must be nourished, nurtured, cared for and loved in supportive, rich and meaningful ways in order to fulfill its destiny.

Chapter Four 47

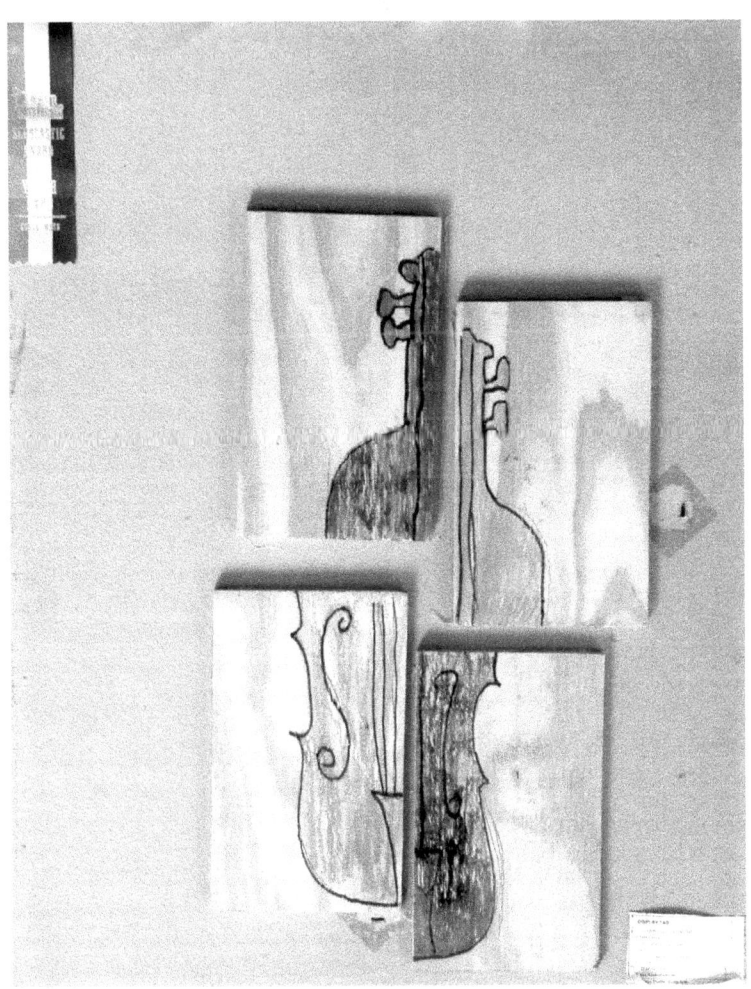

Woodwork Cello by Gabrielle Latimore, Age 7

CHAPTER 5

Be a Parent, Not a Friend!

Let parents bequeath to their children not riches, but the spirit of reverence. PLATO

The following is from a text that a dear friend, who is also a mom, sent to me. We do not know who the author is.

"For as long as I live I will always be your parent first and your friend second. I will stalk you, flip out on you, lecture you, drive you insane, be your worst nightmare and hunt you down like a bloodhound when I have to, because I love you. When you understand that, I will know you have become a responsible adult. You will never find anyone else in your life who loves, prays, cares and worries about you more than I do. If you don't mutter under your breath "I hate you" at least once in your life, I am not doing my job properly."

My daughter is an amazing person, and as she grows and matures, I realize that someday I would very much like to be friends with the adult that she is going to become. I see in her compassion, strength and determination, the same traits I look for all in my friendships. But now, while she is still growing, she needs me to be her mother, not her friend.

When I told a friend of mine that I did not consider myself to be friends with Gabby, she was aghast. She asked me if I meant it, and I nodded firmly.

"There are things that are appropriate for friends but not for parents, and vice-versa," I explained to her. "My daughter is great, but one thing that she needs is firm and clear boundaries. I offer her far, far more than a friend can, and she needs to remember and respect that."

My friend looked at me dubiously, so I explained my thinking to her in greater detail:

"My child lives in a world that can be frightening and confusing. She doesn't always know how to deal with what is going on in her life, and sometimes she feels lost and insecure. I am her parent, and she should always know she can come to me for answers because, more than anyone else, I have her best interests at heart. Even if I do not have ready responses, I will do all I can to find her the answers she needs.

A friend, however, occupies a different place in our children's lives. A friend may be someone that they care about very much, but friendship implies equality. If my children consider me as their equal, their ability to trust me will be lessened, and my ability to give them the help I need to as a parent will be limited."

In recent years, a big controversy has been stirred up by Amy Chua's book *The Battle Hymn of the Tiger Mother*, in which she promotes a high-pressure, high-control style of parenting. This is not what I am advocating, nor am I leaning to the opposite end of the spectrum where I'm best buddies with Gabby. I don't make her my best friend because she is not emotionally or intellectually prepared to play that role.

Boundary Setting Between Parent and Friend

When it comes to making sure that my daughter sees me as a parent and not as an equal, I always think of boundaries. Some people see boundaries as limiting, but I find that they help give me an idea of where to act and what I need to do. Instead of feeling limited by my boundaries, I feel freed by them.

For example, one boundary I carefully maintain is that I do not talk about money matters to or in front of my child. I teach her how to budget and how to save, but beyond that, the money issues and concerns that I have as an adult are none of her business and none of her concern. She cannot process the information or see the bigger picture as adults do. I know that making a careless comment can spark long sleepless nights when my daughter becomes convinced that we're in dire straits when really we just need to stop eating out so much!

Similarly, I keep any disagreements with my husband strictly between the two of us, and he does the same. Gabby needs to see us as Mom and Dad. She does not need to worry about the things that are going on between us, because no matter what, our roles as her Mom and Dad will never, ever change.

Now compare this to what would happen if I allowed myself to think of my child as my friend. Friends are honest with each other, so when I was feeling a bit of a budget crunch, I would tell a friend. If I told my daughter, she might become worried or guilty, and because she is a considerate and generous person, she might think that the onus is on her to scrimp. This is not something I would wish on the child I cherish so much!

If I were in a disagreement with my husband, I would confide in my close friends! I might vent, I might say some things in jest that I did not mean, which might make it sound to a young, inexperienced mind like I was on the verge of divorce. Not only might Gabby take this out of perspective, but it would rock her world to think that her parents were separating!

Even worse, she might feel as if she had to take sides. My friends take my side in disagreements with my husband, but if my child is acting as my friend, just think how bad would that be for her? An argument that ropes in the kids is indirectly asking them to choose, and this is never okay.

Respect Always

I am the parent and my daughter needs to respect me. In many ways, this is to ensure harmony at home, but in a very real sense, it is also about her safety. When you are with a friend, you are with an equal. That means that your judgment is as good as theirs and vice-versa.

However, my child needs to understand that I know best as her parent, and that when I give an order, it must be obeyed. This counts for small things, like when she is told to clean her room, and for large things as well, such as not hitching a ride from a stranger, no matter how convincing he or she is. I provide a structure for her, I set rules, and I reinforce consequences by rewarding positive behavior. These things help her know that I will keep her safe and secure.

For example, I recall an incident many years ago when my daughter was quite small. We were out for a walk and suddenly, an utterly enormous dog came bounding up to us. We didn't know where the dog had come from, and though it didn't look dangerous, I was not taking any chances.

"Honey, I want you to stand very still," I said softly to my Gabby. "Don't turn your back on the doggie, and don't run, okay?"

Gabby obeyed me perfectly, and as the dog looked on in curiosity, I had her slowly back up until she was standing right next to me. I scooped her up in my arms, and happily enough, that was when the dog's owner caught up with it. We exchanged a few words, and with permission, I showed my daughter how to pet the dog.

It doesn't take a lot of imagination to see how that scene might have gone very, very wrong. What if the dog had in fact been a feral stray? What if my daughter, disregarding my words, had run off in a panic? A dog that large and a girl that small are a bad combination. Even a friendly dog could have knocked her down and injured her.

For my child's own safety and my own sanity, I need to be a respected authority in her life. I need her to know that when I speak, she listens. I am not a tyrant, but there are situations when she needs to have faith in me and to trust in my words, no matter what!

Roles Within Roles

I suspect that a sharp parent/child divide often results from roles that are too stiff and unbending. I think it is essential that I understand my child's strengths and the gifts that she has. This does not contradict my expectation that she respect me as a parent at all!

I learn something new from Gabby every day. Sometimes it's a strange new piece of information that she brings home from school, and sometimes, it is something profound that she teaches me just by being who she is.

I respect Gabby for being different from me and for expanding and growing in her own ways. So long as those ways are not harmful, I will help her, and I will learn from her as well.

It's time for another exercise, so take out a piece of paper and a pencil. You can also work on a computer if that would feel more comfortable for you.

Number down the page from one to ten, leaving enough space between each number for you to ink your thoughts as they bubble up.

Now, write down the lessons you have learned from your children today. It might be something that you have learned about the world, or it might be something that they have taught you about yourself.

Let yourself write freely and honestly. If it helps you get started, here are a few from my own list.

"I am more patient than I ever thought I was." "The capital of Mongolia is Ulan Bator."

"How beautiful sitting and watching a caterpillar spin its cocoon can be."

"I can last longer without sleep than I ever thought I could." "YouTube produces instant celebrities."

(This last lesson was prompted by a remark from my daughter, who said, "Some famous YouTuber has 30 million followers. Duh!! Mommy, how is it you don't know who he is? Didn't you go to college?"

As you can see, not every lesson is weighted with meaning; some of them will require a great deal of patience from you, and then again some are just tests to see how hip or cool you are.

However, I can never deny that bringing up my daughter is a learning experience, and a rewarding one at that. When I want to look for compassion, kindness and generosity in action, I am more than happy to look to my own daughter for the lesson. This does not make me any less the parent, and it doesn't undermine my authority; instead, I merely acknowledge that my child is a wonderful person who deserves my respect.

Think about your own children as you make your list. As you do, you will likely feel your respect for them expand and grow. Really understand that that respect can exist within the strong boundaries that contain the relationship between parent and child. There's great freedom to be found in this realization.

Some people think that by avoiding being friends with my daughter, I am sending her a message that she is unworthy. But the truth is that she is worthy of everything I can offer her as a loving parent, and it is only by maintaining these boundaries that I can give her everything I've got.

Maintaining the Peace

As Gabby grows and matures, I am aware that I am pretty lucky. She is on the whole good-natured and obedient. She understands why I do the things that I do, and she is generally willing to take my word on many issues.

My friends compliment me on having such an obedient kid, and I have to laugh at that! Gabby is strong-willed and intelligent, and you only have to talk to her for a moment to realize that she is far from docile!

One of the great things about maintaining the parent/friend divide is that I really do get to make the rules. However, because I am someone who loves my child a lot, I make rules that are good for my kid.

For example, when I became a parent, I promised myself that I would never answer a child's questioning "but why?" with a simple, sharp "Because!"

Gabby is a bright kid, and if something seems amiss to her, she deserves to have an explanation. I might give her a rather short simplified answer, or I might have to say, "That is going to be something we have to discuss later," but in general, if she wants to ask why, I will generally make time to offer her some clarification.

When you know why you are following a rule, it makes the rule a lot easier to follow. For example, if you came in to work one day and there was suddenly a rule that says you could no longer wear the color green, you would likely be quite confused and irritated! You must remember that for children, who are new to the world and do not have your level of experience with it, your rules often sound similarly strange and unreasonable. If they only get a snappish response, they are going to both resent your authority and fail to see why the rule was necessary in the first place.

I have raised Gabby to be a very independent thinker. She knows that when I make a rule, it is for the good of the entire family, and that she is being kept safe by it. I never want her to follow a rule that is arbitrary or needless; as a matter of fact, I think that if she followed a rule unquestioningly, it could be very dangerous for her in the long run!

Instead, I teach my daughter to understand why she needs to trust me, but I also raise her to ask questions. Her questions do not undermine my authority. Instead, they reinforce my understanding that I am raising a child who thinks about the world, who questions what she does not understand and who trusts me to provide her with explanations and solutions, if the situation requires them.

Part of the reason that I do as well with Gabby as I do is because I treat her as an individual and whole human being. She is my child and I am her parent, and she knows and trusts that this relationship will never change. She knows she can rely on me to act in her best interests, and because of that, she needs to put her faith in me and to give me the respect that I am due.

I am also raising a young lady who understands that I cannot be with her at all times to solve her problems. Under my guidance, she is building confidence in her own intuition and decision-making ability, so that she can pick and choose wisely and trust that she has made the best decision for that particular moment.

Chapter Five   57

"Windy Night" by Gabrielle Latimore, Age 7, recognized for Outstanding Artwork and Creativity in Imagination Celebration, Arts Orange County, 2010

CHAPTER 6

It Happened to Me

Children have never been very good at listening to their elders, but they have never failed to imitate them.
JAMES BALDWIN

I don't want you to think that I'm a perfect parent. That might sound a little startling from someone who is writing a book on parenting, but I think that it is always important in a book like this to remember that absolutely no one is perfect.

Every relationship is a work in progress. It is inevitably an exchange. Sometimes I give and sometimes I have to take, and so does the child. I made a sacrifice to scale down on my medical practice when Gabby was two. My reward? I have a child who knows beyond all doubts that she can always count on her mommy.

There was also a side-outcome from that deliberate decision to cut back on my work schedule. I used the time that was freed up to train in trading commodity options, and I am now a profitable trader. I am proud of this skill. It makes money for us and it is something that I can teach Gabby so that she will have many tools at her command to shape her future entirely to her liking. By cutting back on the unrelenting demands of a medical practice, I found other doors opening to me, and we have greatly benefitted from that turn on the road, both Gabby and me.

There are no perfect people, but there are perfect moments. Those perfect moments are times and places where everything comes together just right and you realize why you love being a parent and how much you love your children.

I struggled with perfectionism in parenting for a very long time, and what I found was that instead of always chasing an impossible ideal, I should have just relied on my instincts and my knowledge of my child. Nonetheless, I have stayed firm to the promise that I made when Gabby was two, to learn from her and to be open to the lessons she has to offer me daily about how to raise her.

In the interest of fairness, I want to share what my own parenting experience has been like and pass on to you some lessons that I had to learn the hard way. Some people say that you should never let them see you sweat, but I don't believe that. Parenting is hard work, and it always has been. There are easy days, but there are also days where you will want to tear your hair out. This is why you need to take a long moment, listen to a few of my stories, and think about where you come from.

Summer Camp Adventures

A few years ago, I sent my daughter to summer camp. It was a sleep away camp that was supposed to last two weeks, and when I brought it up with her, she was enthusiastic. It would be a perfect chance for me to get some work done and spend time on projects around the house, and I also thought it might help my daughter become a little more brave and adventurous.

As the day for camp drew nearer and nearer, however, Gabby grew more nervous and timid. She started saying that she didn't want to go, and that she was afraid. I tried to talk to her about it, and I tried to show her all the fun she was going to have, but when I put her on the bus to go, she was shaking and near tears.

I talked to some of my mommy buddies about it, and they said not to worry.

"Soon she'll be having such a good time that she won't even remember being this upset. You'll see."

It sounded like great advice, but then Gabby was calling me up two or three times a day, begging to come home. Sometimes she was angry, and sometimes she was tearful, but the message was clear that she wanted to leave camp immediately.

I was at a loss, and when I talked with my mommy buddies again, they told me that it would pass.

I did my best. I kept our conversations short, and I told her that it would be fine. But she only grew more and more upset, and after a day spent dodging her calls, I had finally had enough.

I gave Gabby a call, and I sat and talked with her for almost an hour. I really listened to what she was afraid of and what she wanted, and I told her how much I cared about her and how much I loved her.

As it turned out, she was feeling very isolated, and it wasn't that she missed being at home so much as she missed me. It made my heart hurt when she admitted that, and we talked some more. I reassured her that I would be here and waiting for her when she came home, and that I always loved her, even when she was far away. From what I could tell, she had overheard me talking with a friend about how much I expected to get done while she was gone, and her young brain had taken that to mean that I was eager to get rid of her!

I reassured her that that wasn't true, not even a little, and that no matter where she was, I would always miss her and want her with me. I told her that if it helped, I would call her every night to say goodnight, and that we could touch base like that.

I called her the next night, and the night after that. After a few days, Gabby informed that she was fine, and would be okay with my not calling so often. I definitely had a little pang in the heart when my little girl said that she would be good on her own, but when I got off of the phone, I was smiling with pride.

Sometimes I shudder to think of what it would have been like if I had continued to ignore her. I was listening to general advice about kids, advice that was not applicable to my daughter in this situation. By not reflecting on my child's specific issues, I wasn't paying attention to her individual needs and to what I knew about her.

As soon as I recognized her needs, Gabby and I could work together to make sure that we were connecting in a deep and real way. It brought us closer, and interestingly enough, it also gave her the strength and security to be more independent.

What I learned from this is that if you want to make your children more independent and self-determining, you must first give them the kind of confidence and security that they require to fly!

It strikes me as funny that I always get a laugh from company when I tell them I have just one kid. Inevitably, the knee-jerk response is that "she must be a spoiled brat." Not at all. My Gabby is not a spoiled brat and I've been very mindful of any tendency to over-pamper her. When she was nine, she was assigned household chores. She sorts through her laundry, I put them in the wash, and she folds her own clothes when the drying is done. This happens every week. She is responsible for keeping her bedroom clean and I check that she fulfills that responsibility. She does the dishes on weekends, unless she needs time to finish a school project due on Monday. She is not paid for chores.

During the week, she is excused from doing dishes to focus on homework. However, she is not exempt from dishes during holidays. She has to wash them every day. I am not saying that Gabby is an ideal child. She protested and complained when the vacation rule was first implemented, but when I deducted money from her Christmas savings on every complaint, she gave in and has since carried out her chores with care.

She earns money by taking care of neighbors' cats. She also earns money from me for babysitting herself – money that would have been paid to the babysitter is now given to her. It was her idea and this is how she conceived it.

On the occasions that I had to work when Gabby was home from school, I would take her with me to surgery. So one day, she came up with a suggestion. If she were to follow me to surgery, I wouldn't need to find and pay for a babysitter. Thus, if she followed me, it stood to reason that she should be given the money, and she was willing to accept a rate lower than the official babysitting rate. On top of that, she reminded me, by having her as a passenger, we would be eligible to drive in the carpool lanes and I would get to work faster. I was struck and pleasantly amused by her strategizing and creativity, and I gladly forked over the money to her.

Gabby is very smart, and I cannot pull wool over her eyes. As such, I reward her for jobs well done, such as earning good grades, to instill in her the belief that she is deserving of the good things in life. I don't always reward for good grades; they are meant as a surprise and I am mindful of any extra effort she puts in to improve from a bad grade the month before.

When we are out shopping and she wants things that I think are frivolous, I suggest that she buys them with her own money. That suggestion usually puts an end to any complaints or whining. Gabby works hard for her money and understands that it has to be earned. As of this writing, she is saving for a fun summer camp and special software for her computer animation and as such will not spend her money freely.

She knows my role as a parent is to provide the best necessities for life and a great education for a bright future. If she wants anything beyond what I am willing to provide, she will have to earn it for herself. My daughter knows beyond a shadow of doubt that I have her best interests at heart, and I always will.

Love Letters from Gabby

> *2009: Dear Mom, I love you. I like you because you are my mommy. I like to play with you because you are so much fun. You are my best mom in the hole wide world. Love Gabrielle*

In 2009, my daughter's love was something bright and shining. She knew I was her mommy, and she knew that we had fun together. Some days, I yearn for the time when Gabby was still that young, though I certainly didn't have that perspective at the time!

This letter paints a very idyllic picture of what we were like and who we were, but you also have to remember that we had our struggles. Sometimes I lost my temper, and sometimes my daughter did, and that could leave us both angry and frustrated for hours at a time.

However, despite this, I was still the best mom in the "hole wide world" and no matter what happened, she still believed it and I tried to live up to the title.

There's nothing as awe-inspiring as the idea that a little child looks up to you with that much unquestioning trust, and sometimes the pressure can be terrifying. It makes you feel as if the weight of the world is resting on your shoulders.

However, each time Gabby smiled at me, and I knew that it was all worth it.

> *2012: Dear Mom, I love you because you take care of me. You help me. You're especially good at loving me. Thank you so much love and care. Happy mother's day!! Love Gabrielle*

Chapter Six

For the first part of my daughter's life, everything was very concrete. I was her mother, and she was my daughter. She felt my love like a plant feels the sunshine, and like a sunflower, she automatically turned her face towards me as my love shone down on her.

Now that she is a little older, you can see that she is realizing what love is and what it means to love someone. She understands that being her mother involves more than just taking care of her daily needs, because it is something that I always do. I take care of her and want the best for her because I love her unconditionally. She has realized that love is a force that moves people, and that it is what ties the two of us so tightly to one another.

She can see love as a kind of gravity, something that gives our lives meaning. This realization means that she is blossoming into her own human being who understands the meaning and purpose of interacting with another person. Sometimes, I miss the tiny girl she was, but every day, she makes me more proud of the girl she is turning in to.

> *2013: I love you mom. I really, really love you with all my heart. There is nothing to keep us apart. Mommy and Gabby. The kisses and hugs you give me make me feel free. I would not ever ask for anything more. I "heart" u!!*

Now in 2013, we're beginning to see a little more of the woman that Gabby will someday become. I was so happy to know her as an infant and a little girl, and now I know that I will be proud to know her as a woman.

She has got fire, and she knows that love is something that you need to fight for. She sees us as a pair, as two people who love each other and through that love can conquer mountains. She realizes now that there is so much that can happen in the world, and she knows that our love will always be a safe place for her.

She understands how serious I am when I talk about love, and how love keeps us stable and gives us the kind of strength that we need to thrive. Gabby is growing into a woman to be reckoned with, and I can't wait to meet that woman. However, I also know how fast time can fly by, and I am not going to object if she wants to stay a little girl for just a little longer.

The truth is that love makes us all better, and if there is a point to this book, it is this. When you move forward with love for your child in your heart, there is nothing in the world that can stop you. Your work as a parent (and yes, I do mean work!) is something that will carry you forward in your life, giving you strength and purpose.

Parenting is a spiritual obligation that I feel I owe to God, the universe and all humankind. I feel it is a duty to raise a human being that will be tolerant and cognizant of the consequences of his or her actions for herself, others, and the planet. This is a duty that I take seriously.

Be willing to take chances, to trust your children and to let them show you the way!

Chapter Six   67

"The Mermaid" by Gabrielle Latimore, Aged 6, displayed at Imagination Celebration, 2009

CHAPTER 7

Becoming a Better You

Nothing has a stronger influence psychologically on their environment and especially on their children than the unlived life of the parent. CARL JUNG

Somewhere along the way, in the process of growing we are told to drop our imagination and grow up! Ironically, inventions that have become part of the comforts of modern life are results of imagination, such as the PC on which I type.

Granted that as a parent, I have to assume a position of leadership. Many a times, this create conflicts and feeling of being unfulfilled as one is forced to abandon childhood dreams. To address this conflict, I had to tap into my intuition as my guide

We all to some degree have limiting belief systems that are results of the way we were raised that impact our parenting skills. Mine was a self-sabotaging habit which came from the belief that I had to work extremely hard for anything worthwhile—that I did not deserve to experience or possess anything good unless I had specifically earned it I once had a hypnotic session and while under trance was able to pinpoint the origin of this belief.

At a very young age, in elementary school, I had come home with a grade that I assumed was great, but not for my grandmother. I took the second position in a class of 30+ kids, and this was not acceptable to her; I had to have the first position. I was 5 years old! And for being second, I was denied a Christmas present that year. So the equation was hard work equals worthiness. Thus started a lifetime of self-doubt and self-sabotage.

Yes, despite getting to the origin of this belief, it took me another 10 years to change it. As a parent, I was determined not to use the same parenting techniques used on me, techniques that I did not agree with, on my child; thus I kept searching for answers. Please understand that old habits die hard, and try as much as I may, there were times I found myself using some of the old learned techniques on my child. It took a lot of awareness not to do that, and that meant getting to a better me.

The epiphany happened when I understood that there is a big difference between capabilities and worthiness.

Capabilities are achievements that portray our abilities.

Worthiness is not associated with accomplishment. It does not need to be earned — it is a divine right and it is your birth right.

We are all born with a worthiness that is infinite and our strong desires are inspired by our infinite selves. From a psychological view, when I tell myself that I deserve something, my consciousness thinks, "Great, let's work for it." On the other hand, when I tell myself that it is my birthright, my universe or infinite self understands it has to find a way to bring it to me because I am worthy of it.

When we allow ourselves to be guided by the infinite self — the universe, your intuition, the subconscious, the imaginary friend, whatever name you choose to use — there is a sense of peace with knowing that anything is possible. So that begs the question, if my infinite self knows that I am worthy of all these great desires, why did I have to struggle?

We are all given the gift of free will, and as an adult and a parent who no longer plays with imaginary friends, we have to choose between the logical ego of our left brain and the sometimes illogical, imaginary all-knowing infinite self of the right brain.

   Once I granted permission to my infinite self to guide me, it was easier to see things from my child's perspective sometimes and easier to resolve conflicts.

   Gabby, has a creative spirit and has on numerous occasions attempted to create new fragrances and experiments out of supplies at home. These are experiments for which I would have been annihilated as a child had I tried them because I was wasting money. When she does these experiments, I look at it from the perspective of its impact on her growth and caution her next time to use smaller portions. Because I recognized another limiting belief from my childhood, I was able to encourage my daughter's curiosity.

   One exercise that readers could do to identify their limiting beliefs would be to take note of the theme of recurring thoughts, especially those that frequently frustrate them or cause them to act in ways that they dislike. Money is usually a big one for lots of people. Thoughts like "man, there are more days in the month than money." Ask the question, why does it feel that way and how can I change this feeling? You can then determine if there is a real problem that needs to be addressed, via visiting a financial planner or more careful budgeting, or of there is a thought pattern from childhood that associates spending money with guilt or fear.

"Violin and Rose" by Gabrielle Latimore, Age 6, selected by Orange County of Education for public display.

CHAPTER 8

Proven Strategies for Becoming Your Best Self

He who cannot change the very fabric of his thought will never be able to change reality, and will never, therefore, make any progress.
ANWAR SADAT, PRESIDENT OF EGYPT

As a parent or even any person in a leadership position, it is easier to lead by examples. This requires making lasting changes within your character that people watching you can emulate. Sustainable changes come from the mind, your thoughts and winning the battle of your mind. Actions speak louder than words.

The battle of the mind — who are the players? As the owner of a one-member corporation, whenever I am asked about corporate officers, my response is, "me and myself and I." There is always that pause and they are probably thinking, "This woman is crazy!" Then I laugh and soon they are laughing also.

Who are me and myself and I? I want to ask forgiveness of readers that do not believe in a higher power. I do. This is not about religion. I am a very spiritual being and definitely not religious, so my family thinks I am a heathen, a very happy one. My foundational spirituality is based on the Bible and I have chosen to interpret the Bible in a way that works for me and my fellow humans regardless of their religious affiliation. Enough said on that topic.

The Bible talks about the "Trinity": God the father, God the son and God the spirit. Me and myself and I. We all have 3 minds:

1. Your conscious logical mind, the soul, the me or God the son, (yeah, I know, blasphemy? God will forgive me).

2. Your subconscious mind, the unconscious, the non-conscious, the spirit, myself or God the spirit)

3. Your pure conscious mind, the "I AM" or God the father, source consciousness, the universe, your infinite self or the higher self.

As the conscious mind has the ability to learn, understand, and rationalize, and emotions are created here. By becoming aware of the thoughts or the movies playing in the background of your mind, you can control what shows up on the screen and your feelings. In other words, you can consciously decide how you will feel by being intentional about how you interpret the situations you encounter. For example, if you are driving at speed limit on the highway, and you see flashing red lights behind you, there are one of two ways to interpret this scenario. One would be to say to yourself, I am good because I am obeying the law. The other would be to panic. I have often found that in my life, option number 2 results in being pulled over as my thought created that reality. So I choose to think happy good thoughts. The same situation can produce two different emotions based on the way I think about it.

The subconscious mind makes no value judgment and is illogical. It understands two things: safety and threat. Its number one job is for your safety and survival, your " fight or flight response."

The subconscious mind is what drives you. More than 80% of the mind is in the subconscious mind. This is where change has to take place if it is to be effective. The subconscious operates through energy. The energy associated with any event is what drives the subconscious. Joy, gratitude, sadness or anger are some examples of the energy or frequencies understood by the subconscious.

The energy with which you approach any task will determine the subconscious perception of threat or safety, so changing the energy you bring to a task is the way you affect change. The big one for everyone is money. The benign innocent habit of complaining about lack of money could result in the subconscious seeing money as an object of threat. Since its number one job is to protect you, it keeps money away. To change this, adopt a habit of gratitude for even a penny on the street and soon you will be finding dimes, quarters and Benjamin Franklins.

Approaching parenthood from a place of joy, with a spark of curiosity, and fascination with the new things that your child is capable of doing each and every day will let the subconscious know that parenting is fun and will in turn bring more of positive energy. I am always amazed at the myriads of untapped potential of the human mind whenever I see my kid learn a new skill. I am just like wow, I wonder how much more that I am capable of doing if I stretch my imagination a little bit.

I used to have a hard time saving screen shots and would always ask my kid. Her response to me one day was, "If I show you, you will never remember, and if you figure it yourself, you will never forget," Yep, she was right. Now I know, you press the little window key and the one that says "prt sc" and the screen will dim briefly and viola. No one had ever explained this principle of learning to my daughter, but it is a perfect example of the wisdom that children are capable of.

The pure conscious mind is wisdom and knows. Have you ever had the feeling that you know something, but your conscious logical mind cannot articulate how it is that you know it — you just know? This is your pure conscious mind. This is your true self, the one that is capable of unconditional love you have as a parent for your child. This is the part of you that is capable of forgiving regardless of how many times they have disobeyed you. This is the you that will do anything for your kids. Living from this place is what makes life fulfilling.

This is where conflict arises — when there is incongruence between the three minds, or "me and myself and I." For example, say I am using positive affirmations about my financial situation, and a bill arrives in the mail. One part of me wants to revert back to insufficiency and think, "Where is the money going to come from?" I just declared to my subconscious that I do not believe I have enough despite my positive affirmations, thus manifestation is delayed.

If you have ever read Napoleon Hill's *Think and Grow Rich*, he describes the "invisible counselors method." He would visualize a meeting among himself and several individuals whom he highly respected and wanted to emulate. Well, me and myself and I usually have to have an executive meeting so we can have integrity and congruence among us.

The "I AM" gently whispers to you to have faith and "walk on water" so to speak, to let go of the past and take a chance. Myself, (the subconscious) whose main job is for my safety, will promptly bring up memories and remind me of the need for safety and why I should remain in the comfort zone. The conscious logical me will concur with myself. Thus I remain in my uncomfortably predictable comfort zone with the same habits that no longer serve me. After all, the safety of my comfort zone is that it is predictable.

So please ask yourself, what habits do I have from the way I was raised that I am now using on my kids and no longer serve me?

Unresolved issues will be reflected onto our loved ones, especially kids. This is why there are certain generational "curses" that seem to linger within families until there is one brave soul, aka " the black sheep," who dares to do otherwise.

Develop a habit of having regular executive meeting with all 3 of you, in my case, "me and myself and I." This is easier said than done, no doubt. It requires a conscious effort.

Living in LA, my commutes are long, so this is where I hold my executive meeting. Hey, fortunately people use their Bluetooth and speaker phones a lot, so when I have my meeting and am visibly speaking out loud to "myself and I," I look perfectly normal. I don't look like I am crazy. We crack each other up and have a good time.

Most importantly, "me and myself and I " all come to an agreement on what is safe for me. You see, my subconscious is only concerned about me, not my loved ones. It does not know my loved ones. The memories created are from my personal experiences. Take the time to identify what each part of yourself would say and decide which direction to go. You could even add to the meeting and, like Napoleon Hill, imagine seeking and getting advice from admired figures with character traits you would like to emulate. This is where sustainable change happens and it is, believe it or not, effortless.

To change the memories that are programmed into my subconscious, I need to rewrite the emotions related to the memories. We create our reality not by what we think, but by how we feel. Your feelings create your reality. Emotion is energy, and energy attracts like energy.

Everything is vibration, and you attract that to which you resonate.

You can create something more quickly when you believe in it, love and cherish it. The energy given to anything determines the results obtained.

If my desire is to have a great relationship with my child, I get excited at the thought of hearing her laugh, seeing her happy and successful in life. I imagine that I have a great successful happy little girl and I literally get excited at seeing her get happy over getting an A+ .

When your mind is focused on thoughts that are filled with joy, peace, love, abundance and feeling successful, there is a good feeling and you are in vibrational harmony with your desires.

Feeling and attitudes that create a higher vibrational frequency are happiness, bliss, appreciation, love, joy, gratitude, certainty, peace, admiration, faith, courage, hope, freedom, and trust.

On the flip side, feelings that create lower vibrational frequencies are condemnation, guilt, worry, resentment, fear, disappointment, hesitation, sadness, insecurity and doubt.

Unhappiness is the lowest state of vibration that you can resonate at. There is a feeling of depression, being overwhelmed, boredom, anger, heaviness and helplessness. Life is full of gloom and doom, rain and darkness and this is the reality that is created. These are the people to whom the saying, "if it wasn't for bad luck, they won't have any luck at all" is applicable.

The middle state is monotony. This individual is on auto-pilot and do things because they should do them, almost robotic. The world is cloudy and boring and the results are "same old thing."

The highest state is joy. This individual is alive and on fire. They have excitement about everything. When you vibrate at this level, even when things are tough, you just choose to see the positive in everything. Your life is full of good cheer and sunshine and you operate from desires and inspiration and naturally effortlessly attract your heart's desire.

Newton's first law of motion, sometimes referred to as the law of inertia, is often stated as

"An object at rest stays at rest, and an object in motion stays in motion with the same speed and in the same direction unless acted upon by an unbalanced force."

Choosing to be happy and focus on positive thoughts, imagining the excitement, the joy, the gratitude and exhilaration you will feel to manifest your desire now, will actually put you in a happy emotional state and make manifestation happen even faster.

Imagining your child suddenly becoming this incredible great kid will change the way you can interact with them.

Please understand that sometimes there are negative feelings that are cause for action. By thinking about what you can do to change that negative feeling if it is real, or letting go if there is not much that you can do about it, will allow you to move to a higher vibrational frequency to better manifest your heart's desires. The flight or fight mechanism is there for your safety, so be careful not to let go of common sense and use it when appropriate.

A consistently high vibration leads to faster manifestation. We generally feel better about something the more excited and emotionally charged we are about that desire, and therefore, the faster that desire will show up. Interestingly, the excitement about manifesting a desire in one area spills into other aspects of your life. It is contagious!

Sustainable change translates to a fulfilling experience as a parent, and I am affecting the next generation through my parenting and leadership role.

There is a point in life when the roles will be reversed and the child will return the favor and become the parent. Isn't that something? The parent that you are to your children is the parent that they will be to you when the roles are reversed. Life is a self-fulfilling prophecy and you do reap what you sow. Be the parent you will want your children to be when roles change.

I am grateful to "me and myself and I " for their collaboration on this book.

80   Parenting with a Twist

"Cheese, Wine and Grapes" by Gabrielle Latimore, Age 6, selected for display at the Orange County Youth Expo

Bonus

As a valued reader, I would like to invite you to receive a complimentary parenting personality assessment. This bonus as my way of thanking you. I want to share with you a tool that I personally used to become a better me and in turn a great parent to my kid.

With this bonus, you will receive a one hour personal profile consultation with me valued at $280.

To get your bonus personal profile go to
http://www.parentingwithatwistbook.com/bonus

Conclusion

The child supplies the power but the parents have to do the steering. BENJAMIN SPOCK

If you look at my biography below, you'll see the long list of titles and degrees that I hold. I am proud of all of them. I love being a medical doctor, a trained anesthesiologist, a life coach, and a public speaker. All these things enrich my life in different ways, but what you must remember about me is that the title I am the most proud of is 'mommy.'

As soon as my daughter took her first breath, I knew that I would be her mother until the day I die, no matter the twists and turns life lobs at us. It doesn't matter to me whether I am watching her take her first steps, getting ready for prom or dressing up for her wedding. She will always be my daughter, and I will always be her mother.

Some people take this as a kind of burden, and some women have even taken me to task for "limiting" myself in this way.

They think that because I proudly declare myself a mother, I cannot possibly have anything else going on.

When people tell me this, I can only laugh! All I can think about is all of the wonderful experiences I have enjoyed and the lessons I have learned because I was a mother. I have been led down confusing and wondrous paths that I would never have taken if my daughter had not come into my world.

If I leave you with anything, let it be this: that there are so many ways to be a good parent. Parenting magazines go into great detail about different parenting styles, and there are books in the stores that scream out about Parenting Gone Bad. I am not against any of the ideas and tips that these books offer. However, I distill my view of parenting into a simple conclusion: Parenting doesn't end until you take your last breath. However, as long as your parenting style involves understanding your children and guiding them towards being complete, confident, authentic human beings, you are going to be swell at the job and have fun along the way too!

I have opted to take a long road to fulfillment and purpose. Sometimes, I must admit, it is easy to get frustrated when things don't quite go as planned. However, adopting a flexible mindset is part of the joy. Even when I am having a rough day where everything seems like it is going wrong, I always know that I would never trade being a parent for anything else.

While Gabby's unique personality has largely determined my experience of parenting, I think that even if I had had a different kind of child, I would still be just as committed to growing on this path. I would be learning different lessons and becoming intelligent in different ways because I would be dealing with a different personality, but my interactions with my child would still teach me how to learn and grow. I just need to make sure I am open to learning those lessons, rather than rigidly committed to a system of parenting that does not take into account my child's and my own individuality and continual growth.

Life does not travel in a straight line, and no matter what you think about it, it can take you anywhere. I have decided to use my role as a mother as a compass. It informs what I do, and it allows me to detect where the truth lies in many situations. I make decisions with greater awareness of their repercussions, not just for me but for the little person who depends on me.

I also see parenthood as an opportunity to learn. Gabby is sensitive and she reminds me how much I needed compassion in my own youth. I see many adults who hurt as easily as she does; the only difference is that they know how to hide it a little better. I know when someone is hurting, and I know how little it takes to make the world right for them again.

On top of that, I have also learned how to be tough. The world doesn't always play nice, and sometimes it feels like people have it in for girls just like my daughter. They tell her that she's unworthy, that her interests are dumb and that she's silly. I've taught my daughter that she is strong, and I have taught her that she is worthy of respect, but when the world knocks her around, I am always by her side.

When you are a mother, you learn very quickly how to stand up for yourself and how to make sure that you are strong for your children. I found this strength within because of Gabby, but it hasn't remained focused only on her. Everyone who knows me knows that I am a fighter, and they know that I do not stay quiet when there is a wrong that needs righting.

These are just a few of the lessons that I have learned, and I know that I will always cherish them. Being a mother has taught me how to be a better person, and it has absolutely shown me how to be kinder, stronger and fiercer than I ever thought I could be. They say you should never come between a lioness and her cubs. Yes, as mothers, we are women who roar.

Where are you at on your journey? How do you see your role as a parent? So many people see parenting as a role that consists mainly of responsibilities that need to be discharged for twenty minutes at the beginning or at the end of the day. However, I have chosen to embrace my role as a parent more deeply, knowing that my life is much richer because of it.

The only titles I had prior to my daughter's birth were MD and anesthesiologist. Ironically, at a time when I should perhaps have stopped pursuing further education because I now "had my hands full" as a mother, I actually became more enthused about my work. This enthusiasm stemmed from a renewed curiosity about how the brain develops. Watching a helpless newborn evolve into a little being who could independently lift her head and roll onto her back really got me curious.

This curiosity encouraged me to challenge myself and led me to ask what other potential I might have lying dormant in me that I have not yet explored. Of course the next question that naturally follows is what do I actually want?

Here is my challenge to you: What excuses have you given yourself for not having achieved some of the goals and desires you have for your life and invariably for your children? I have been very fortunate to have had many great teachers in life. My Gabrielle is the best of them all.

Reflect on the lessons that I have discussed in this book, and think about whether they apply to your own life. Being a good person is something that requires conscious work, but when you let your child be your compass, you can be secure in the certainty that you are heading in the right direction. Don't be afraid to wholeheartedly embrace this role. Don't sweat the small stuff, don't worry about how you are going to be perceived by others, and don't worry about any rough spots that may lie ahead, trusting that you'll have the strength to face them when they come.

Are you ready to take the next step on your journey? Being a parent is not something that simply happens when your child is born. It is also something that you work on and invest in. The life that you live is a shaping influence on your child, and the reflection they show you will in turn shape you.

Conclusion

Let your role as a parent transform and change you into a wonderful person. Children are just the beginning, but the journey you start with them can lead you deep inside yourself, as well as out in the world. Remember, the apple does not fall far from the tree. You are your only limitation! Dare to think outside the proverbial box.

I am a mother, and I know that my journey has only just begun.

About the Author

Dr. Blessing Akpofure, MD prefers to be called Dr. Blessing, and the name is spot on for the people she has helped! She received her MD from Georgetown University School of Medicine, after earning a B.Sc in biology and a minor in child psychology from George Washington University in Washington DC. Upon graduating from medical school, she spent a year at The Martin Luther King/Charles Drew Medical Center in Los Angeles as an intern in trauma/general surgery. She completed residency training in anesthesiology at the University of Miami/Jackson Memorial Hospital in Miami, Florida. She is also licensed to practice medicine in the states of California, Florida and New York.

As a result of her fascination with people, she also received certification in Ericksonian Hypnosis and Neuro-Linguistic Programming. She is certified in Neuro-Linguistic Programming and Neurological Repatterning, and in presentation and platform skills (known to sensible people as public speaking). She also works as a performance consultant and a results-oriented life coach.

Dr. Blessing is also collaborating with veterans to create the non-profit organization Rejuvet™, geared at housing vets and creating self-sustenance.

As a mother, she believes in a life of self-sufficiency and is learning how to profitably trade futures, forex, and options. She is also teaching her daughter, who is fascinated by how you make money on the Internet, how to trade.

90 Parenting with a Twist

Award for "Windy Night" from Imagination Celebration, Arts Orange County, 2010